Seasons

What Can You See in
Winter?

Siân Smith

Raintree

Raintree is an imprint of Capstone Global Library Limited, a company incorporated in England and Wales having its registered office at 7 Pilgrim Street, London, EC4V 6LB – Registered company number: 6695582

www.raintreepublishers.co.uk
myorders@raintreepublishers.co.uk

Text © Capstone Global Library Limited 2015
First published in hardback 2014
The moral rights of the proprietor have been asserted.

Edited by James Benefield and Kathryn Clay
Designed by Richard Parker
Picture research by Tracy Cummins
Production by Helen McCreath
Originated by Capstone Global Library Ltd
Printed and bound in China by Leo Paper Group

ISBN 978 1 406 28324 2
18 17 16 15
10 9 8 7 6 5 4 3 2

British Library Cataloguing in Publication Data
A full catalogue record for this book is available from the British Library.

Acknowledgements
We would like to thank the following for permission to reproduce photographs: Getty images: Jim Arbogast, 11; iStockphoto: © PamelaJoeMcFarlane, 18; © ParkerDeen, 7; Shutterstock: ayosphoto, 20 left, Beata Wawrzyniuk, 16, BestPhotoStudio, 19, Bobkeenan Photography, 13, Brykaylo Yuriy, 9, 22, Franck Boston, 20 right, gorillaimages, 12, Monkey Business Images, 5, newphotoservice, 6, back cover, Pavel L Photo and Video, 20 middle, Pi-Lens, 14, RDaniel, 10, 22, Richard Schramm, 21, romakoma, 17, Triff, 4, 15, Zurijeta, 8

Cover photograph reproduced with permission of Shutterstock, Kotenko Oleksandr.

Every effort has been made to contact copyright holders of material reproduced in this book. Any omissions will be rectified in subsequent printings if notice is given to the publisher.

Contents

Things you can see in winter

You can see snow.

You can see snowballs.

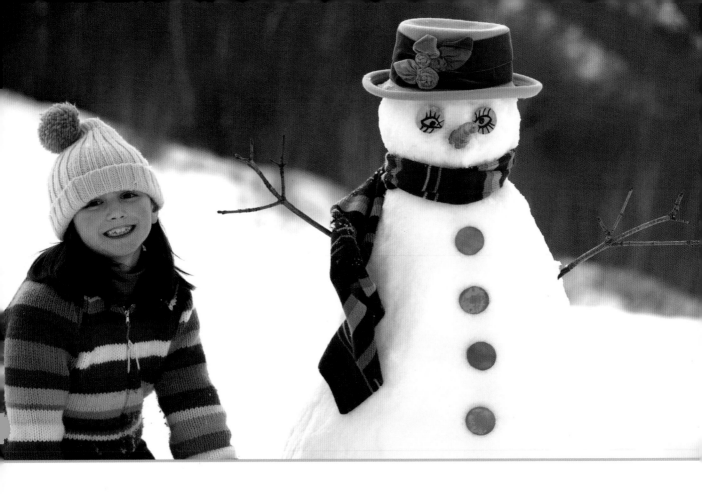

You can see a snowman.

shovel

You can see a shovel.

You can see sledges.

icicle

You can see **icicles**.

You can see **ice skates**.

You can see hats.

You can see gloves.

You can see holly.

You can see snowploughs.

You can see bare trees.

You can see wreaths.

You can see lights.

You can see hot chocolate.

You can see soup.

Winter quiz

Which clothes would you wear in winter?

The four seasons follow a pattern. Which season comes after winter?

?

summer

winter

autumn

Picture glossary

 ice skates

 icicle

Index

Answer to quiz on page 20: hats and coats
Answer to question on page 21: spring

Notes for teachers and parents

Before reading

Building background: Talk about the seasons of the year. Which season are we in at the moment? Ask children what they would see if they looked out of a window in winter.

After reading

Recall and reflect: Which season is before winter? Which season follows winter? What is the weather like in winter? What is the best thing about winter?

Sentence knowledge: Help children count the number of words in each sentence.

Word knowledge (phonics): Turn to page 10. Ask children which word starts with /y/. Which word starts with /s/? Which word starts with /i/?

Word recognition: Ask children to point to the word *see* on any page. Ask children to find the word *see* on other pages.

Extending ideas

Make a snowflake: Give each child a square of white paper. Fold the paper in half to make a triangle. Fold the triangle in half again to make a smaller triangle. Position the triangle with the point down. Fold in each side towards the point. Cut off the top of the folded paper at an angle. Now cut out large shapes from the sides of the triangle. (Children may need help with cutting as the folded paper is thick.) Ask children to open up the triangle to reveal their snowflakes. While making the snowflakes, ask children to identify shapes.

In this book

Topic words
gloves
hats
holly
hot chocolate
ice skates
icicles
lights
shovels
sledges
snow
snowballs
snowmen
snowploughs
soup
trees
wreaths

Topic
winter

High-frequency words
a
can
see
you

Sentence stem
You can see _____.

Ask children to read these words:
hats p. 11
gloves p. 12
hot chocolate p. 18